25 WAYS TO
RELEASE
THE
GREATNESS
IN YOU

RANDY D. WRIGHT

PURE PRAISE PUBLISHING

29193 NORTHWESTERN HWY

SOUTHFIELD, MICHIGAN 48034

25 Way To Release The Greatness In You

Copyright© 2012 Randy D. Wright

ISBN-13: 978-0-9740877-5-7

CREDITS
Cover Design and & Layout
Larry T. Jordan, Pure Praise Media

EDITING AND PROOFING
The Sound Proof

May be purchased in bulk for educational use. To order books, please send an email to: designer@purepraisemedia.com and include your contact information.

PUBLISHED BY:
Pure Praise Publishing
29193 Northwestern Hwy, Suite 573
Southfield Michigan 48034, USA

www.purepraisemedia.com
designer@purepraisemedia.com

Printed in the United States of America

Table Of Contents

PART 5 - PASSING ON YOUR GREATNESS

Acknowledgements

To my wife Darlene, thanks for believing in me and standing right by my side. You are truly a woman of greatness, special love, patience, talent, and abilities. I love you.

To my mom Catherine Wright Hall, no son could ever hope for a greater, more loving, and more caring mother than you are. You have been a great inspiration to me. I love you Mom.

To my sisters Beatrice, Rosie, and Kathy, and my brother Ron, each of you hold a special place in my heart. We have shared so many wonderful life experiences together. You are the greatest family a brother could ever want. I love each of you so much. Thanks for all of your support. James Williams (brother-in-law), thanks for being just like a brother to me.

To my editor Ron Johnson, thank you for bringing your expertise to this project in order to bring out the best in me. You challenged me to push myself a little further and to write more from my heart—and I did.

To Larry Jordan, you are my mentor and friend. You helped make this book a reality. You helped me to see the greatness in me by your words of wisdom, enlightenment, and encouragement. Thanks for believing in me and going through the process of becoming an author with me. You are a great man.

To my PR coach Pam Perry, you are a talented and extraordinary woman whose coaching skills, patience, valuable information, and expertise super exceed the call of duty. Your PR Boot Camp gave me the hunger and drive to succeed. Your hands-on training, assignments, and accountability helped me to see the preparation it takes to become a published author. Anyone who is coached by you can't help but to be great!!! You go the extra mile. My life has been changed because of you, Pam. Thanks Coach.

To all my nieces and nephews, Alesha, Nell, Vonnie, Tramaine, Sharita, Nedra, Noga, Oneshia, Eternity, Kaneshia, Tamika, Tiffany, Tanice, Tamara,Ladeshia, Regina, James, Ronell, Christopher, Reshard, Charles, Troy, Day Shawn, Rodney I, Rodney II, Trevon, Devon, Al, Stephen and La Ron I love you all.

To the (late) Uncle Charles and Aunt Eloise Simpson, and Uncle Hubert Brown, as well as all of my aunts, uncles, cousins, and godchildren, I love you all.

To Kevin and Gwen Parish, you are two of the most special people in my life. Thanks for proofreading and giving me a lot of encouragement to finish the book—what a great couple.

To Marilyn Toaster and my mentee Bradley Toaster, your proofreading and encouraging words helped me persevere until the book was complete. Special thanks to my mentee Courtney Whitty for helping me with so many projects.

To my childhood mentor and role model Rich Wood, who made the difference after my father died, you helped me to be a man and work through so many problems.

To Dale Bishop, thanks for helping to release the greatness in me by being a part of the YFC family and receiving the opportunities to touch so many young people's lives. You have displayed greatness as a friend, brother and employer.

To Mr. Stacey Foster and Dottie Foster, you are two of most giving and precious people I have ever known. You mean more to me than you can ever imagine. You have made a difference in my life. Thanks.

To Daryl Ounanian, you are a great friend and brother. You display greatness by example. Thanks for letting me be a part of the Westside CA family.

To Ken Urban, you are a great man who I admire and am glad to call a friend. Thank you for the role you played in helping my book become a reality. I can write better because of you.

To Jeff and Shirley Wallace, thanks for the wonderful love and support you have showed Darlene and me. Greater things are yet to come for the both of you.

To Hal Davis, you are one of my favorite people. You have such a big heart and have made a lasting impact on me for life. Thanks brother.

To T. J. Hemphill, you are a one-of-a-kind multi-talented person who is also my mentor. Your mentorship has helped me see the greatness in what you do by paying attention to details. Thanks.

To Kenneth and Debbie Anderson, you are two of my favorite people who invested in me a long time ago. I never forgot what you did. Thank you.

To Marty Bulgar, Dr. Jay Marks, Harvey Wilson and William four outstanding men who impacted my life and so many other young men at Project Manhood. Thanks for letting me be apart of the team at Southfield High School.

To Edna Williams of Oak Park Youth Assistance who is a sister and good friend. You are making a difference.

To the (late) Terry Barr who had such a powerful impact on my life not only as an employer but a mentor and a person who cared about people

To Alan and Michelle Barr, Rick Felstow and Valeria Warren who are all special people who enchanced my greatness.

To Jenny Morgan, Julia Ward, Brenda Roach, Lisa Morrison, and Marja Winters you all are very special women who I have enjoyed working with.

To Ken Marshall, Daryl and Rhonda Winters. Thanks for being good friends.

To all of the youth I presently work with or have ever worked with, thank you for being such a special part of my life. All of you are like my children. Your greatness and uniqueness are what drive me forward. I love all of you.

- Randy D. Wright

Introduction

Why I wrote this book

Have you ever felt stuck, depleted, and tired of doing the same things over and over again, with little or no fulfillment in your personal or professional life?

This book was written for those who dare to step outside of the everyday grind and choose to live an extraordinary life. A life that is not limited to being average or normal, but a life that chooses to be "great!"

25 Ways to Release the Greatness in You was written to give you direction, motivation, and inspiration to do great things with your life.

Greatness is not about money, possessions, or power—it's about fulfillment. It's about releasing the hidden talents, gifts, and abilities that are inside of you to change your world and influence the lives of others.

As you read this book, beginning with Chapter 1, use it to "think big" and discover your unique purposes, thus releasing the…Greatness in You.

Randy D. Wright

PART 1

GREATNESS IN
THE MAKING

CHAPTER ONE

Greatness Starts the Moment You Decide to Think Big Enough

"When you decide to think big enough, you can achieve a worthwhile goal or dream that burns in your heart day and night."

–Randy D. Wright

Greatness starts the moment you think big enough to become great. Begin now to think big enough to accomplish whatever you want to do, have, or become.

Greatness is a force that burns inside your heart to release your own unique talents and abilities.

Greatness refuses to be average or ordinary.

Greatness is the awareness that in order for you to fulfill why you were put here on Earth, it must be discovered and achieved.

I know what it means to wake up every day and want to pursue a life that's not average or ordinary. I know what it means to want to release the greatness inside of you, in order to make a positive impact and to contribute to the life of others, but not know where to start. I want you to realize right now that there is greatness on the inside of you—bottled up, lying dormant, just waiting to be released. You can become all that you desire to be if you just take this journey to release your greatness now.

Think bigger than your current circumstances.

Think bigger than your adversities or foes.

Think bigger than your present losses.

When you think big, you unlock your dreams and possibilities. You give yourself permission to succeed.

I challenge you to believe that with faith, tenacity, and perseverance, you can do the unthinkable. Accomplish the impossible and become unstoppable!

DARING TO THINK BIG ENOUGH

Janice Bryant Howroyd had a vision of greatness that started while she was working for her brother-in-law at Billboard Magazine in Los Angeles, California. Janice noticed that most of the employees who worked there did it just for money, while waiting to break into the entertainment business.

Janice also noticed that she enjoyed helping people get temporary and permanent employment. Through this system, someone encouraged her to start her own company. Janice listened and took her savings of $967 along with a loan of $533 from family members, and used it to start Act 1 Personnel Services in Beverly Hills, California.

DOING THE IMPOSSIBLE

Janice Bryant Howroyd not only had the challenge of being a female business owner, she was also one of the few African-American female business owners. She stepped out and did the impossible by running her own company.

Faced with rejection, doubt, and skepticism by

large and small competitors, Janice decided to move forward. She said, "I grasped the dream and created a reality for myself, and in so doing gave opportunity and value to others."

Janice built her reputation by guaranteeing to find and send only the most qualified employees or return the payment. With this commitment to excellence and greatness, Janice Bryant Howroyd's company earned $10 million in just a few years.

Her original investment of $1,500 has turned into a $500 million business. Today, her company has ninety offices nationwide, 290 full-time employees, and is the largest African-American female-owned employment service in the country. That's greatness.

ANSWER THESE QUESTIONS

You, too, must dare to think big and achieve the greatness that awaits you. I want you to start this journey by answering the following questions:

1. What dream burns in your heart day and night?

2. What are you willing to do, learn, or become to achieve this dream?

3. Is your dream a part-time fantasy or a full-time burning passion?

4. What is the significance of your dream and what rewards will come from accomplishing it?

Once you answer these questions, it's time to move on to implementing a vision and a plan.

CHAPTER TWO

Developing Your Greatness with a Vision and a Plan

"Vision is a process that allows you to think ahead to where you want to be and what you want to be doing, and to create a plan to get there."

—Fred Pryor

Your vision is like fuel to a fire. It ignites and takes off on its own—once it is written out in detail. Without a vision and a plan, you lack direction and order. There is no way you can give substance to your dreams or make them become a reality.

1. A vision is a vivid picture created by your imagination, where anything is possible.

2. A plan is an organized, detailed blueprint of the ideas, goals, and dreams that you have put in writing, with a specific date or time to be completed.

The main reason why a lot of people don't release their greatness is that their vision and plan is in their heads and not written down on paper.

You will never give great significance to your vision, unless it is written down. I can't tell you enough about the value of writing down my vision and plan, and how it has helped me. When an idea or goal comes to my mind, I immediately write it down or record it on my digital recorder.

I get ideas and plans sometimes at the strangest moments and in the oddest places. I get them before I go to sleep or at three o'clock in the morning, but I grab my ink pen and write them down and go back and review them later.

My goal in this chapter is to get you to make a commitment to put down in detail (i.e., plan) where you are headed (i.e., vision). Don't rely on your memory alone.

A MAN OF VISION

Thomas Watson Sr. was a man of vision. He built IBM (International Business Machines) into the world's largest manufacturer of electric typewriters and data processing equipment.

Watson's road to greatness started with many ups and downs. He attempted to become a bookkeeper, but quit. He sold organs and pianos, but this was not his vision either.

After leaving the organ and piano business, Watson joined the National Cash Register Company as a salesman, and eventually was promoted to general sales manager. He excelled and even impressed John Patterson, the company's owner and founder, with a sign that read, "Think."

Mr. Patterson ordered copies of the sign for all of his offices. Due to a dispute over antitrust legal issues, Watson left National Cash Register and became president of Computing-Tabulating-Recording Company.

Watson was forty years old when he took over as general manager of this small firm, which manufactured an assortment of tabulators, time clocks, and meat slicers. He changed the name of the company to IBM.

During his forty-two years at IBM, Watson pioneered the development of accounting and computing equipment that is used today by the government, scientists, businesses, and various other industries.

When Watson was near the end of his life, he was asked the following question: At what point did you envision IBM becoming so successful? He simply replied, "At the very beginning."

People with vision know what they want, devise a plan to achieve it, and expect to obtain positive results. Napoleon Hill, author of Think and Grow Rich, said, "Cherish your visions and dreams as they are the children of your soul, the blueprints of your ultimate achievements."

ANSWER THESE QUESTIONS

That is what I want you to do. Cherish your visions and dreams and release them through your plan, which is the blueprint to your success.

1. What is your vision?
2. What is your plan to carry out your vision?
3. Write out in detail a start date and completion date to achieve your goals that are attached to your vision.

Here is a sample vision statement you can use to create your own.

Within the next five years, the Women's Center will have helped create a safer, more harmonious community by helping women acquire the education, skills and resources necessary to build self-sufficient prosperous lives.

The goal is to have a Women's Center. Five years is the target date for completion. The vision statement is how it will be carried out by providing education, skills and resources necessary to build self-sufficient and prosperous lives.

CHAPTER THREE

Discovering Your Unique Purpose

*"Greatness is knowing you were born for a purpose
and that you have fulfilled that purpose, by using every
talent, gift, and ability given to you by God."*

−Randy D. Wright

Greatness is more than talent and abilities. In order for you to fulfill your greatness, you must have a purpose. Many talented and gifted people exist today, but most of them never reach their full potential. They get stuck on trying to be great, instead of preparing to be great.

One of my mentors made an impression on me with the following statement: "The quality of your preparation will determine the quality of your performance." It's your responsibility to prepare yourself to achieve your potential. Every person will have opportunities throughout their lifetime to express or display their talents and gifts to others.

It is in the preparation stages of your life that you practice, train, develop, and sacrifice to push yourself to the limit. Washington Irving said, "Great minds have purposes, others have wishes. Little minds are tamed and subdued by misfortune, but great minds rise above them."

DISCOVERING THE POWER OF YOUR PURPOSE

On a cold winter night, standing on the shores of Lake Michigan, ready to jump into the freezing waters, a thirty-two-year-old bankrupt and jobless man, who had just lost his daughter to complications from polio and spinal meningitis, reflected on the emptiness of his life.

Ready to commit suicide, a thought flashed through his mind. Should he end his life? "No" was the answer that came back to him.

You do not have the right to end your life. You are responsible for grabbing hold of it and contributing to changing the world and benefiting all humanity.

This is how Bucky Fuller discovered his unique purpose, as he turned his back on the deadly waters of Lake Michigan and set out on a remarkable career. His decision not to end his life has changed the lives of many people.

He is best known as the inventor of the geodesic dome—a building that could sustain its own weight with no practical limits. It is the lightest, strongest, and most cost-effective structure ever devised.

Bucky went on to become a world-famous engineer, mathematician, architect, philosopher, and poet. He held more than 170 patents before his death in 1983.

Bucky discovered his purpose by understanding that tragic moments should not cause one to give up on life. So, don't ever give up on yours. Life is a journey. Take it one day at a time.

UNDERSTANDING YOUR PURPOSE

Discover what your unique purpose is and why you are here. Begin by asking yourself the following questions:

1. What am I most gifted and talented in doing?
2. What drives or motivates me?
3. How can I develop myself to acquire the necessary skills to turn this gift or talent into a service or product?

Once you answer these questions, write out a plan of implementation. Again, this will serve as a necessary blueprint to helping you fulfill your unique purpose. Don't be like the lazy servant in the Bible (Matthew 25:16–25) who buried his gift, refused to develop it, and made excuses for not getting a return on his master's investment. You have a lot to offer. The world needs to see your greatness.

You are responsible for discovering and understanding your unique purpose. Don't waste a lot of time doing nothing—like most people. Instead, spend your time planning and preparing for the extraordinary days ahead.

CHAPTER FOUR

Overcoming Limitations and Obstacles

"Obstacles stimulate us to uncover dormant abilities. Out of difficulties comes new strength."

—*Unknown*

A couple of things that come to stop you when you make up your mind to release your greatness are limitations and obstacles.

Can you identify what is stopping you from reaching your greatness? What limitations are you allowing yourself or others to impose on you? What obstacles are blocking, delaying, or stalling your progress in releasing your greatness?

- Limitations are simply restraints that try to stagnate or confine your progress in reaching your maximum potential.

- Obstacles are sometimes temporary roadblocks that appear to be insurmountable problems.

- Limitations and obstacles are sometimes hidden opportunities.

- Never let limitations or obstacles stop your creativity.

UNLEASHING YOUR CREATIVITY

Charles Darrow was a salesperson during the Great Depression. When his sales position suddenly ended, he began doing other odd jobs to make a living. At night, he used his creativity to work on a board game that several people could play at once.

Darrow presented his game called Monopoly to Parker Brothers, who turned it down because they said it violated some sacredly held principles. They also thought it was too long, too complicated, and had no clear-cut finish.

The rejection of Parker Brothers didn't stop Charles Darrow. He decided to produce the game on his own, with the help of a friend who was a printer. It was a success.

Wanamaker's was the first company to purchase Darrow's idea. They sold 5,000 games the first year. Parker Brothers realized the success of Monopoly and reconsidered Darrow's offer. They made a deal with him to purchase the game. Through heavy marketing, sales escalated to 20,000 units every week.

Because Charles Darrow used his creativity and didn't allow the limitations and obstacles of Parker Brothers to stop his dream of greatness, he became the world's first millionaire game designer.

Never underestimate the power of your creativity during hard times. What invention, product, or idea do you have now that could solve a problem or bring fulfillment to others if it is released into the marketplace? This invention, product, or idea could make you very wealthy.

Sometimes the greatest inventions and ideas are birthed through seasons of limitations and obstacles.

Seize the moment now to unleash your greatness. Let's reflect once again on what could be hindering your ability to release your greatness.

1. Can you identify what is stopping you from reaching your greatness?

2. What limitations are you allowing yourself or others to impose on you?

3. What obstacles are blocking, delaying, or stalling your progress in releasing your greatness?

4. What are some ways you can go beyond your current limitations and struggles to pursue your greatness?

I want you to focus on the top three to six goals you must reach in the next thirty days. Who are the people, contacts, or companies that you can schedule an appointment with to discuss your ideas?

Write a proposal explaining the details and benefits to these people, contacts, or companies. Have an attorney go over your proposal to make sure it's a win-win for all involved.

CHAPTER FIVE

Do Something Special with Your Life

"In this life we will encounter hurts and trials that we will not be able to change; we are just going to have to allow them to change us."

–Ron L. Davis

Now is the day, now is the time for you to do something special with your life. You have unlimited potential inside of you to change your world. Releasing your greatness is a call to action. It's having the mindset to transform unsatisfying circumstances into dreams of reality.

WANTING TO CHANGE

Three young men from Newark, New Jersey, who were the best of friends since grade school, experienced hard times growing up on the streets in the eighties. One of them, Sampson Davis, served time in juvenile jail for armed robbery; and his friend, Rameck Hunt, was incarcerated for attempted murder.

The experience really had an impact on Rameck Hunt, who vowed not to spend his life that way after he was released. Another friend, George Jenkins, and the other two young men talked about the many negative things they witnessed in their neighborhoods. The thing that stands out the most about them is that they decided to do something special with their lives.

George, who had a dream of being a dentist, met a recruiter who visited his science class and talked to him about the possibility of attending college at no cost. But there was a catch. In order to attend college for free, George had to go into the medical field. He wanted to convince Sampson and Rameck to do it also.

This was a big challenge for George, but he was willing. After convincing Sampson and Rameck, the three friends made a pact to apply to Seton Hall University and go to medical school together. Then, all three guys got rewarded with scholarships to Seton Hall.

Despite having to overcome trials and temptations along the way, Rameck Hunt, George Jenkins, and Sampson Davis made it through. These three young men are a testimony that you can overcome bad surroundings, the streets, failure, defeat, and setbacks by deciding to win.

Today, Dr. Sampson Davis is an emergency room physician; Dr. George Jenkins is a dentist; and Dr. Rameck Hunt is an internist. Oprah Winfrey called the three doctors "the premier role models of the world." They have written two books on the New York Times best-seller list called The Pact and We Beat the Street.

They have received many honors and accolades, but they will tell you that the real reward is making a difference in the community.

What are you waiting for? You are special. You can change the direction of your life right now. Decide today that this is it! Nothing can stop you. You're going to do something special with your life. You're going to make a difference. You're preparing for greatness. Now, just go do it!

PART 2

DEVELOPING A
NEW MINDSET

25 WAYS TO
RELEASE
THE
GREATNESS
IN YOU

CHAPTER SIX

Position Yourself for Greatness

"The people who are playing it totally safe are never going to have either the fun or the rewards of the people who decide to take some risks, stick out, do it differently."

—John Akers

Someone once said, "You've got to be in position for success to happen. Success doesn't go around looking for someone to stumble upon." Greatness is the same way. If it is placed within your reach, you have to put yourself into a position to attain it.

How do you put yourself into a position to release your greatness? How do you know what looks like an opportunity or a lost cause? What if you fail? What if the pain of obtaining greatness is far greater than the reward? Then, what do you do?

I believe the answer is found in a quote by Michael LeBoeuf, Ph.D. He said, "The greatest single determination of what you will be or do with your creative abilities is your perception of who you are. Self-esteem is central to the whole problem of securing any type of success in any endeavor." I totally agree with Dr. LeBoeuf. It's only by how you perceive yourself that can you expect to position yourself for greatness. How do you see yourself? Do you like you? It's all about how you see yourself. Your self-esteem is what counts the most. Raise it to a higher level.

Begin today to release yourself from whatever has been holding you back. Release yourself from carrying the baggage of any hurt, pain, turmoil, or loss that has long held you back. Release yourself from feelings of self-doubt and unworthiness.

You are somebody special. You are someone that is just as good as the next person, but you have to believe that and receive it in your heart.

Positioning yourself for greatness means you must take an active role in preparing yourself for it. Greatness won't happen just because you want it to. It is an on going process that requires you to give of yourself, even if it means sacrificing and delaying some other things you want to do right now. It's about prioritizing.

You may need to upgrade your skills. Take a college course, learn a trade, or become an entrepreneur by starting your own business. Whatever you need to do, it's time to position yourself for success.

POSITIONING FOR GREATNESS

How do you put yourself into a position to become a member of an NBA World Championship team? No one would have ever believed it could happen for a six-foot-seven-inch, 145-pound point guard named Scottie Pippen.

Scottie Pippen attended the University of Central Arkansas, a small NAIA college. He was a non-scholarship player who received financial aid for being the team's work-study manager.

To pay for the rest of his education, Scottie worked in the summers as a welder, attaching school desk arms to their legs. In his freshman season, he didn't impress anyone, as he averaged 4.3 points a game. He decided to position himself to learn and prepared by working hard and improving his basketball skills.

By his senior year at Central Arkansas, Scottie averaged 23 points and 10 rebounds a game. He became a hot commodity in the 1987 NBA Draft.

Even though his chances were slim at first, Scottie Pippen didn't quit. He knew if greatness is placed within your reach, then you have to reach out and grab it. His consistent practice and preparation made him ready when the opportunity came.

Pippen positioned himself to be drafted by the Chicago Bulls, where he played alongside Michael Jordan. Scottie would later become a seven-time All-Star, eight-time NBA All-Defensive First team member, and a six-time NBA Champion. Scottie Pippen is an example of how you should never stop positioning yourself for greatness.

How are you positioning yourself for greatness? Could it be that a person you already know might be the golden connection that you have been waiting for? You will never know unless you set aside your presumptions and position yourself for it.

REPOSITION YOUR THINKING

Early in my career, I was given an application by my friend for a new job. I took the application and set it on top of the refrigerator for thirty days, because the pay was too low and it was too far to drive.

Due to unforeseen circumstances, I had to "reposition" myself, because my current employer was letting the entire staff go in two weeks. I finally decided to fill out the application. Little did I know, this new job turned out to be the biggest break I could ever hope for—it thrust me into my greatness.

I received three promotions in six months. I was chosen as one of the top seven employees to go through their fast-track program, where I was trained all around the United States to become a top executive. I was able to thrive with this organization because I repositioned my way of thinking. I didn't let a thirty-minute ride to work dampen my expectations to succeed. I wanted to succeed. I worked long hours; I took seminars and special training to increase my value to that company. And it paid off.

Sure, there were some rocky roads. Some people even questioned my rapid promotion. But I never let that stop me. I ignored their negative words. I persevered in spite of their rough treatment and criticism. I was determined to express who I was by giving, 100 percent of my time, talent, and skills to make that company a success. I did it. I repositioned myself.

I took that opportunity and let it change me. It stretched me; it built confidence in me. It showed me that when some people oppose you, there are other people who care about you and are willing to help you.

Are you looking at the opportunities to reposition yourself? If not, I encourage you to stop and take another look. The right opportunity could already exist. You just have to position yourself for it. Unlimited possibilities could be surrounding you, but you may not be aware of them.

Greatness could be placed within your reach disguised as something else. Open your eyes and take that leap of faith. The best is yet to come, when you position yourself for greatness.

1. What opportunities could you be over looking to reposition yourself?

2. What person or place of employment already exists but you have not recognized it as an opportunity?

3. Stop and take another look at every relationship personal or business that could position you to release the greatness in you.

CHAPTER SEVEN

Delaying Immediate Gratification

"We live in a world where people want instant results, immediate gratification, without long-term commitment and hard work."

–Unknown

A student once wrote to a famous preacher named Henry Ward Beecher, asking him how to obtain an easy job. Surprised by the student's request, Beecher replied, "If that is your attitude, you will never amount to anything."

NO EASY JOBS

He explained to the student that any of the professions he desired to get a job in—editor, lawyer, minister, politician, medical professional, or merchant—were not easy jobs.

Mr. Beecher went on to say, "My son you have come into a hard world. I know of only one easy place and that's the grave."

We live in a world where a lot of people don't have the patience to delay immediate gratification. They want it now and if they don't get it, they become impatient, frustrated, bored, and ultimately settle for less.

What about you? Are you looking for an easy job? Are you willing to settle for less so you don't have to exert any great effort on your part? If you are, don't be surprised with the results.

Success is a series of small achievements. Success is about doing the little things that you don't want to do, in order to become great. Great dreams come with a great price.

You must be willing to go through the process. There are no shortcuts. Only by gaining valuable knowledge, wisdom, and experience can you expect the gratification that comes with greatness.

The grave is full of people who died and never developed their greatness. Some were geniuses who never graduated from high school. Others used their wits to con and take advantage of people because they wanted to get paid—now! Yet they never fulfilled their greatness.

The world will never know the difference that these people could have made. Nobody will ever know the legacy that they could have left for their families, had they been willing to delay their quest for instant gratification.

1. How much time are you willing to sacrifice daily, weekly or monthly to acquire the skills, and resources necessary to build the life you want to live now?

2. What ways can you show more patience and restraint in delaying immediate gratification?

Make a long term-commitment to follow through on your plans and ideals. Whether it's buying a home, starting a business or getting married think longevity.

MAKING A COMMITMENT TO GREATNESS

Make the following affirmations to yourself on a daily basis:

- I will not be impatient with the process of developing myself for greatness.
- I am willing to apply myself to obtain the necessary skills and develop good work habits for creating the life I want to live.
- Time is my friend, not my enemy.
- I will not lose hope when my dreams are delayed or deferred to a later date.
- I know who I am. I will complete what I started, and become the best possible me.
- I will leave a legacy for future generations.
- I am great. I will do great things with my life.

With this kind of attitude and determination, nothing can stop you. In the words of Zig Zigler, "I'll see you at the top."

CHAPTER EIGHT

Start Each Day Believing That Greater Opportunities and New Beginnings Await You

"We are all faced with a series of great opportunities brilliantly disguised as impossible situations."

—Charles R. Swindoll

Starting over again is often very difficult to do after a failure or a loss. Yet all great people possess a special quality that allows them to look beyond their current situation and have the courage to try again.

LEARNING TO START OVER AGAIN

Starting over again can also cause you to look at a situation from a different perspective. The current economy has forced many people to start over again due to layoffs, unemployment, foreclosures, bankruptcy, divorce, and the loss of 401(k)s and other retirement monies. Here is where you have to ask yourself some tough questions so that you can create a new beginning or discover hidden opportunities.

First and foremost, will you let your present circumstances stress you out? You have to start each day believing that greater opportunities and new beginnings are waiting just for you.

I often tell people, "It's not how you start, but how you finish." Whatever you may be trying to accomplish with your life today, failure should not be the final result. Every new beginning starts with an ending. The only way to reach for new opportunities is to be challenged with the exit of leaving situations and circumstances that no longer work. Failure sometimes can be the hidden stepping stone that moves you toward releasing the greatness in you. Why?

- Failure can teach you many valuable lessons in life.

- Failure should give you confidence to try again, because success is a series of small achievements.

- Failure happens to everyone.

- Failure is actually a process of winning.

Consider the following failures of people who became great.

FAILING INTO GREATNESS

Twenty-three publishers rejected Dr. Seuss's first children's book. The twenty-fourth publisher sold six million copies, and Dr. Seuss died knowing his perseverance resulted in entertaining, challenging, and educating millions of children.

Charles Goodyear, founder of Goodyear Tires, was obsessed with the idea of making rubber unaffected by extreme temperatures. His years of unsuccessful experimentation caused bitter disappointment, imprisonment for debt, difficulties with family, and ridicule from friends. Yet he persevered and in 1939,

Goodyear discovered that adding sulfur to rubber achieved his purpose. He became a success. Failure didn't stop him.

Alex Haley, one of the most successful writers of the 1970s developed his writing interest while in the Navy. For eight years, he wrote a myriad of routine reports with no national success. Little did he know that when he returned to public life, he would go on to write a book called Roots that touched the world. Alex Haley and Roots made history. The book was later turned into a made-for-TV series and held one of the highest ratings for a short mini series ever.

Paul Ehrlich, a chemist, discovered a drug to treat those afflicted with syphilis and named it "Formula 606," because the first 605 tests were failures.

PURSUIT OF A NEW BEGINNING

As a young woman, Sally Jessy Raphael aspired to land a permanent position in broadcasting. However, she found more failure than success. No one in the United States would give her an opportunity. They said she wouldn't be able to attract an audience.

Sally paid her way to Puerto Rico and then flew to the Dominican Republic, where she covered and sold her stories. Once back in the United States, she pursued her passion. But after being fired eighteen times, she wondered if she should reconsider pursuing a career in broadcasting.

Her break finally came after persuading an executive to hire her, even though he wanted her to host a political talk show. With no political experience, she used her conversational style and invited people to call in. They loved her show.

The program was a hit. The networks realized it, and the rest is history. Sally Jessy Raphael would later go on to win two Emmy Awards as host of her own television talk show, reaching eight million viewers daily throughout the United States, Canada, and the United Kingdom.

Sally Jessy Raphael understood that true greatness can be achieved no matter how many failures you encounter in life. All you have to do is be willing to start each day believing that greater opportunities and new beginnings await you.

The same can be true about you. No matter how many failures you may have had, believe in yourself. Be willing to start over again. Failure is not final. Use it as a stepping stone to greatness.

CHAPTER NINE

Character, Courage, and Competence

"All of our dreams can come true—if we have the courage to pursue them."

Walt Disney

Character is a distinctive quality or attribute. No matter how great you desire to be, always remember that with greatness comes great responsibility. Character can be defined as the moral excellence or reputation of a person.

Your character includes not only your reputation, but also your name. You might ask —what's in a name? Proverbs 22:1 of the King James Version of the Bible says, "A good name is rather to be chosen than great riches …"

A person may accumulate great riches and become world famous, but once their name has been tainted—no matter how rich they may be—it doesn't mean a thing.

Your name is really all you have to tell the world who you are. Never take your name or character for granted.

COURAGE AND COMPETENCE

The late President John F. Kennedy reminded us that "courage is the ability to conquer fear or despair."

Courage can also be defined as the mental strength to persevere through difficulty.

- It takes courage to become great.
- It takes courage to leave your comfort zone.
- It takes courage to conquer fear.
- It takes courage to stand against people who doubt whether or not you can become great.

You don't know how many times I have had to overcome negative opinions and remarks from people who didn't understand my true purpose of becoming great.

I don't want to be great just to have people say I'm great. I don't want to be great just to be famous and make a lot of money—neither should you.

I want to serve and give my life for the cause and purpose of helping you discover your talents, gifts, abilities, as well as find the courage to release your greatness.

I want to help others who have had to suffer setbacks, got a late start in life, or were turned down by those who were more educated and influential—those who didn't think they had what it takes to know they are still great. All it takes is competence.

Competence is being capable, efficient, and able.

TURNING COMMON IDEAS INTO GREAT REWARDS

The following people were competent in discovering their true greatness.

- The inventor of Q-tips, Leo Gerstenzang, conceived the idea when he saw his wife trying to clean their baby's ears with toothpicks and cotton.
- Madame C. J. Walker became interested in hair

care products for African-American women, and began working on a hot comb and her "Wonderful Hair Grower." She also founded a beauty school that trained cosmetologists in the use of her products.

- King C. Gillette was inspired to create disposable razor blades after having a conversation with the inventor of soda pop bottle caps.

- Ole Evinrude, while rowing a boat and eating ice cream that melted on his way to a picnic spot, got angry. So, he invented the outboard motor to get to a place with speed.

- Charles Strite invented the automatic pop-up toaster when he was upset by the burned toast in the factory lunchroom where he worked.

Great ideas sometimes come from meager beginnings. Remember that it's all about character, courage, and competence. These qualities will launch you into your next level of greatness.

CHAPTER TEN

Become the Best at What You Do

"You create opportunity. You develop the capacities for moving toward opportunity. You turn crises into creative opportunities and defeats into successes and frustration into fulfillment."

—Dr. Maxwell Maltz

If you have ever watched TV's reality shows, you have probably seen people prepare to become "America's Next Top Model," strive to be the "American Idol," or dance it out for the mirrored trophy on "Dancing with the Stars, " all in hopes of getting that big break into stardom. Isn't it funny how sometimes people are just waiting for a big break or someone to give them a chance?

WAITING FOR OPPORTUNITIES

In spite of all the glamour and glitter on these shows, it all comes down to who will be voted the winner. Rarely does anyone make it all by themselves.

I have entered contests before, competed in sporting events, and auditioned for music and acting producers. I even became a part of a recording artist's group who made a $30,000 video. I also paid a fee to audition as a singer in a contest. But I never got that big break.

Then, it dawned on me. I was leaving my success in

the hands of other people who really didn't know me. They didn't know the desire, drive, or tenacity that I had to succeed with my talents and gifts. That's when I decided to start my own business. I started writing and producing songs, plays, motivational speeches, and inspirational poems.

I decided to create opportunities for myself, instead of waiting for somebody to give them to me. That's one of the reasons why I wrote this book. I wanted to share my experiences with others in order to enlighten and encourage them—and let them know that it's time to release their greatness.

Stop waiting for somebody to give you an opportunity; become so good at what you do that you create opportunities. People will begin to seek you out. They will call you, hire you, and want whatever you have to enhance their companies or make their lives better.

CREATING OPPORTUNITY

What do you think of a child who loved cookies so much that, at the age of thirteen, she took the money from her part-time job and used it to buy butter, vanilla, and chocolate chips to make cookies? Debbie Fields was that child. She eventually started her own cookie business at twenty-one years old.

WHO WANTS A GOOD COOKIE?

Debbie's strongest belief, which turned Mrs. Fields cookies into a household name is, "Never settle for just good, who wants a good cookie when you can bite into a mouthwatering one?" She took her cookies to the extreme. Debbie discovered how much butter she could put in them before it would be considered too much. She found out how much chocolate she could put into the dough until it couldn't hold anymore. She made her cookies with only the highest quality ingredients so no one could compete with them.

Debbie knew that the door of opportunity only knocks for those who are willing to become the best at what they do. Becoming the best to her meant that if she made the best product or offered the best service, she didn't have anything to fear from the competition.

So she made the best cookie possible. Today, Mrs. Fields cookies are sold in over 1,000 outlets in eleven different countries.

You have to develop yourself for greatness every day of your life. Is opportunity knocking at your door? How will you answer it?

Here are a few suggestions:

- Don't settle for being average.
- Don't settle for just being good enough.
- Don't allow laziness or procrastination to stop you.

Dare to stare mediocrity in the face. Decide to become the best at what you do. The door of opportunity is waiting just for you.

PART 3

RELEASING YOUR GREATNESS

CHAPTER ELEVEN

A Dream to Become Great

"Nothing is as real as a dream. The world can change around you, but your dream will not. Responsibilities need not erase it. Duties need not obscure it. Because the dream is within you, no one can take it away."

—Tom Clancy

More often than not, greatness starts with a dream. A dream comes from deep inside of you. Even though you may have a strong desire to fulfill it, you need to know some of the odds ahead of you in your quest to make your dream of greatness come true.

THE ODDS OF BECOMING GREAT

- Becoming great means you have to overcome adversity and endure hard times when all is stacked against you.

- Becoming great means you have to keep believing in yourself, even when it looks like you're not going to make it.

- Becoming great means that those closest to you may not be able to understand why you want to become great.

- Becoming great may cause critics to call you

selfish and question your motives for refusing to be average and ordinary.

- Becoming great may cause doors of opportunity to be closed in your face.

- Becoming great may cause you to be passed over for a promotion, even though you were next in line.

In spite of all these things, none of them can ever stop the person who has a "dream to become great."

A DREAM OF GREATNESS

There was a young man named Joseph who had a dream of becoming great. Joseph was the eleventh of twelve sons born to Jacob, who was written about in Chapter 37 of the book of Genesis in the Bible.

One day, Joseph shared the dream he had of becoming great with his brothers. After he told them about the dream, they hated him. His brothers couldn't understand why he thought that he would become great and rule over them.

Not long after his first dream, Joseph had another dream; but this time he told the dream to his parents and his brothers. His father questioned him and said, "Shall your mother and me along with all of your brothers one day bow down to you and you become greater than us?"

Because of this dream, his brothers envied and hated him even more. But his father kept it in his heart.

ROADBLOCKS TO THE DREAM

One day, while Joseph was at home, his father sent him into the fields to check on his brothers, who had a way of getting into trouble. While Joseph was still a distance away, his brothers noticed him and said among themselves, "Here comes this dreamer. Let's kill him and see what happens to his dreams."

Reuben, his older brother said, "Let's not kill him, but throw him into a pit." Reuben did this in order to buy some time so he could come up with a plan to save Joseph and take him back to his father. So they took Joseph and threw him into a pit.

While the brothers sat down to eat, a traveling caravan of Ishmaelites came by. Judah said to his brothers, "What will we gain if we kill our brother and cover up his blood? Let's sell him to the Ishmaelites and not lay our hands on him. He is our brother." So they sold Joseph for twenty pieces of silver and he was taken to Egypt.

FROM A DREAM TO A NIGHTMARE

When Joseph arrived in Egypt, he was bought by Potiphar, who was Pharaoh's captain of the guards. The Bible says the Lord was with Joseph and gave him success in everything he did. Soon Potiphar realized the Lord was causing Joseph to succeed. So he put him in charge of everything he owned. The only thing Potiphar had to concern himself with was what to eat.

Not long after that, Potiphar's wife approached Joseph and asked him to sleep with her. Joseph refused her. He said,

My master has entrusted everything he owns into my hands and no one in this house is any greater than I am. The only thing he has withheld from me is you because you are his wife. How could I do such a wicked thing and sin against God?

She kept begging Joseph day after day. He refused to go to bed with her or even be with her.

One day, when Joseph went into the house to attend to his duties, he was alone. None of the household servants were inside. But Potiphar's wife grabbed hold of

Joseph's coat and said, "Make love to me!" Joseph ran out of the house with her hanging onto his coat.

DREAM DELAYED

When she saw him run out of the house and leave his coat in her hands, she cried out to her servants and said, "Look! This Hebrew has come here to make fools of us. He tried to rape me, but I screamed and he ran out of the house and left his coat."

Potiphar's wife decided to keep the coat until her husband came home. She told Potiphar the same story she told the servants. Potiphar became very angry with Joseph and put him into prison. He was placed where the king's prisoners were kept.

It seemed like Joseph's dream was coming to an end, but God was with him. God showed Joseph kindness and caused the prison warden to favor him. The prison warden put Joseph in charge of all the other prisoners.

DREAM TO REALITY

Later, the chief butler and chief baker offended Pharaoh. They were put into prison as well. After being in custody for a while, the butler and baker each had a dream the same night. They woke up sad the next day. Joseph asked them, "Why are you sad today?" They explained to him that they both had a dream, but no one to interpret it. Joseph said, "Does not interpretation of dreams come from God? Tell me your dreams."

They told Joseph their dreams. Each dream represented three days. The butler went first: He explained that he held three branches full of grapes and squeezed them into Pharaoh's glass. Joseph said that in three days Pharaoh would restore him to his position.

The baker got excited and told Joseph his dream. He

said, "I was carrying three baskets of bread on my head and the birds came and started eating the bread." Joseph told the baker that in three days Pharaoh would cut off his head and hang him on a tree and the birds would eat away his flesh.

In three days, the dreams happened just as Joseph predicted. The chief butler was serving the king his drink and the baker was executed and hanged. Little did Joseph know that being put into prison would give him an opportunity to be used by God to interpret the dreams of Pharaoh's butler and baker.

A DREAM COME TRUE

Two years later, Pharaoh had two dreams and was very troubled by them. He called for all of his magicians and wise men to interpret the dreams. None of them could. The butler came forth and reminded the king of when he was angry with him and the baker. He told of how a young Hebrew man interpreted their dreams. The dreams came true. Pharaoh summoned for Joseph from prison. This led to his interpretation of Pharaoh's dreams.

Joseph gave Pharaoh a fourteen-year survival plan of how to deal with the great famine that would come from the two dreams. Joseph was promoted to governor of Egypt. His power and leadership was only second to Pharaoh's. So Joseph's dream did come true; he was later reunited with his father, forgave his brothers, and took care of them all.

A DESTINY OF GREATNESS

Joseph could have cried, complained, and blamed God for his misfortunes, but he didn't. He took every experience and learned from it. Even though he was hated by his brothers, sold into slavery, mistreated, lied on, and falsely accused of raping Potiphar's wife, Joseph stood the test.

That's the same thing you have to do to become great. You must stand the test. This is not the time to lose your courage. This is not the time to back out of a deal; this is your time to keep going forward.

Build your own business and set a new standard of excellence. Raise your level of leadership and influence to the status of greatness. You have a destiny to fulfill. Stop looking back at what you could have been and realize who you are becoming now! All the pain, heartache, and suffering will be worth it. Never underestimate who God created you to be.

- Now is the time to demonstrate your greatness.
- Now is the time for you to rise above the rest.
- Now is the time for you to carry out your vision and purpose with a sense of urgency.
- Now is the time for you to "release your greatness."

Sometimes, when your dreams are tested, delayed, or distorted, it makes you wonder if your dreams will ever come true. I know. I've been there, too.

Today, I want to encourage you that no matter how bad life gets; no matter how many dark days you have to go through; no matter how many battles, struggles, and temptations you have to fight; no matter how impossible your situation may be, just keep the faith and realize that God is with you and YOU CAN MAKE IT!

If you put your trust in God, it will cause you to succeed wherever you are. Don't doubt or get discouraged because of where you are right now. Just excel, grow, develop, and mature into the person you were meant to be. This will cause you to fulfill your dream of becoming great.

CHAPTER TWELVE

Giving Maximum Effort to Achieve Maximum Results

"No matter who you are or what your position you must keep fighting for whatever it is you desire to achieve."

−George Allen

Have you ever heard somebody say the following things?

"I wish I was great."

"I want to be number one."

"That looks easy; I bet I could do that."

Yet they never advance beyond their wishes. Some people look at great people and think it's so easy.

DESIRING TO BE GREAT

Many people never become great because being average is normal to them.

- The average person says, "At least I tried," and stops there.

- The average person complains about other people getting job promotions, while they remain at the same position for years. Why? Because the average person may hesitate in taking additional classes to upgrade mediocre skills.

- The average person refuses to volunteer for more than is required of a job.
- The average person doesn't plan and prepare to achieve maximum results.

You can tell it in conversation when the person makes statements such as:

- "He's lucky and always gets all of the breaks."
- "Why is she doing more than the company is paying her for? I know I wouldn't do it!"
- "I don't have time to take classes. I'm too busy."

If you want to be on the cutting edge in the twenty-first century, you are going to have to give maximum effort to get maximum results. Little effort is going to produce little results.

A DREAM OF BECOMING GREAT

When I was in middle school, I had dreams of being a professional basketball player. I loved watching Dr. J, Rick Barry, Dave Bing, and Bob Lanier play basketball. I will never forget trying out for the basketball team. On the first day of practice, the coach had us run seventeen laps around the gym, and then ten times up and down the stairs. I can honestly say this was not my idea of what basketball was all about.

I thought the team would be working on shooting the basketball, dribbling, passing, and playing defense—not running. But I did it, and afterward, I went home and fell out. Guess what? I never went back to another practice. I quit! I gave up!

Why would I give up on my dream of so desperately wanting to be an NBA star? Well, I wasn't willing to give that dream maximum effort. I wanted it to come easy with little effort.

I wasn't willing to push myself. I just wanted the glory of being a great basketball player with no pain or sacrifice of my time and energy. I just wanted to play basketball.

At the time, I didn't realize that my coach had us running all those laps and climbing stairs to condition our bodies. He was preparing us to build stamina and endurance for game situations. I was unwilling to train and prepare.

Merlin Olson said, "One of life's most painful moments comes when we must admit that we didn't do our homework, that we are not prepared."

Many people go through life never grasping the opportunities that are in front of them. They are always dreaming of becoming, but never reaching the point of making a commitment to prepare first. You will never experience the joy of attaining the goals and dreams you have set for yourself unless you are willing to prepare, first.

Why is it that some people never fulfill their greatness? Is it because they lack opportunity? Or is it just bad luck? Is it fate, laziness, or procrastination? Is it that no one ever gives them a break?

Today, I want to challenge you to stop wishing you could be great. Not achieving greatness has nothing to do with bad luck or the fact that no one ever gives you a chance. You have to deliberately give maximum effort if you want to achieve maximum results. Push yourself to the limit and take your life to a level that exemplifies order, prestige, and success. All great people do.

CHAPTER THIRTEEN

Pursue What You Love to Do

"Pursue the things you love doing, and do them so well that people can't take their eyes off you."

—Maya Angelou

What do you love to do? What do you like to talk about all the time? What motivates or inspires you? When you wake up every day, what is it that you long to be?

Releasing your greatness encompasses pursuing the things you love to do. Following are some things that I love to do:

- I love to write.
- I love to motivate and inspire others.
- I love public speaking.
- I love helping people discover their purpose in life.
- I love teaching leadership skills, life skills, business skills, and biblical skills to leaders, youth, adults, and business people.

BUILDING YOUR LIFE AROUND WHAT YOU LOVE

Success in life should be built around what you love to do. When you really love what you do, nobody has to pump you up all the time, or drag you out of bed each day. Nobody consistently should have to say, "Come on, it's time to get going to build the type of life you want to live."

No, you have to be self motivated, disciplined, relentless, and tenacious—and have a passion that supersedes the pain and struggle that comes with success. Here is a reality check to test if what you love to do is something you should pursue in a greater capacity.

1. Have you ever started something in this area, but then stopped?

2. Does your focus, or attention span, only last for a little while when doing this, then you are off to the next best thing?

3. Do you have a hunger and drive that pushes you to be or do whatever it is you want to accomplish in this area, because you can't live without doing it?

If you answered "yes," to the third question, this is probably something you love do. Pursue it.

Norman Vincent Peale was approached by a young man one day who wanted to start his own business. To his dismay, the young man had no money. Mr. Peale replied to him, "Empty pockets never held anyone back. Only empty heads and empty hearts can do that." What you love to do must come from your heart.

Warning! This does not mean that if you want to become a recording artist you should go out and quit your job today. If you love to sing, you should create a plan of action that centers around making a career of it.

Too many people take loving what they like to do to the extreme. They leave careers that provide a comfortable living for their families and then wonder why they are in a crisis. They often miss golden opportunities to learn new skills and advance at their current employment. Timing is everything.

Remember this: To pursue what you love to do doesn't happen overnight. It's a learning process. Proper planning should precede what you love to do. Never jump out of a plane without a parachute. You are bound to crash!

CHAPTER FOURTEEN

Six Reasons Why You Need a Mentor

"The best of all things is to learn. Money can be lost or stolen, health and strength may fail, but what you have committed to your mind is yours forever."

—*Anonymous*

I have seen many people, young and old, make major decisions without seeking the advice of a mentor. They failed. They made huge mistakes that could have been avoided if they had consulted with a mentor. Some of them were unwilling to learn. Some of them didn't realize that nobody succeeds by themselves. You need a mentor, somebody who has gone before you and can show you the way.

WHAT IS A MENTOR?

Mentors are people who have conquered problems and overcome opposition, struggle, disappointment, and pain. Mentors can teach you and help you avoid a lot of pitfalls and mistakes that they have made. The true key to mentorship is your willingness to learn.

IN NEED OF A MENTOR

My father died of cancer when I was fifteen years old. I come from a family of five children and a wonderful, loving mom. I had a really good childhood up until his passing. I felt lost, hurt, disappointed, and even angry because my dad was gone. There were so many questions I wish I could have asked him that pertained to life and how to be a man. There were a few men in my life like Uncle Hubert and Uncle Charles; my eighth grade teacher, Mr. Laramie; Mr. Hill, my principal from middle school; and Rich Wood, a guy from Youth Guidance who my mom had called one time because I was skipping school and getting into trouble.

It wasn't until Rich Wood took me to this camp called "Pines Hills" that I understood, for the first time, what a mentor was. Rich was a good mentor. He believed in me. He led by example; he instructed me and taught me good morals, values, and principles. He was a good family man. And he loved the youth. I wanted to be just like him. Even when I became an adult, he still mentored me and guided me through the process of making some tough decisions concerning my life. He is one of my favorite people in the world. I really love him for his patience and mentorship.

After I got married, I lost contact with Rich for a while. But he showed up at my house one day and asked me if I would volunteer to work with him at a middle school—mentoring other young men. I was ecstatic! You better believe I wanted to volunteer and mentor other young men. I believe just as someone has mentored or poured into your life, so should you do the same for others.

This was actually the beginning of one of my purposes in life. God took the brokenness, hurt, and pain that I experienced from losing my dad and used it as a purpose for me to help other young people who don't have fathers. A lot of young people whom I mentor today may have fathers, but they are not active in their lives.

I have the wonderful opportunity to invest in these young men—teach, instruct, and build positive relationships with them and their families. Most of all, I explain to them: "Just as I have mentored you, I need you to mentor others." This is important to me. The ability to give back and help others who need somebody, have suffered a loss, experienced a setback, or feel stuck in life, and show them the way is what being a true mentor is all about.

A MENTOR IN THE TIME OF CRISIS

There once was this young skier who did not take heed to a danger sign. He felt, since he was an excellent skier, nothing could really go wrong. He decided to ignore the sign and ski in the area. About a week later, he woke up in the hospital with a permanent spinal cord injury.

The young man realized that he would never walk, run, drive a car, or do any of the other things that most teens do. He would never be able to go to his senior prom, work, get married, and have children. He would be confined to life in a wheelchair. Just living this type of life was devastating and stressful to this young man, who was in constant pain, feeling like his life was over.

Family and friends would come to visit him, but his bad attitude and condition was too much for them, so they stopped coming. He felt completely helpless, hopeless, and full of despair. One day, this old man in a wheelchair came to see him and crashed right into his bed on purpose.

The older man yelled, "Whoops!" and introduced himself to the younger man. His legs had been lost in a car crash. After listening to the young man's self-pity story and constant complaining, the older man asked him what he was going to do about it.

The older gentleman shared his own struggles, frustrations, and disappointments with the young man. He challenged him to leave his worries behind and get on with his life.

He encouraged the young man to join his wheelchair basketball team. At the time, the young man didn't know what to expect. He was hesitant, but he was open to learning something new. On the first day of practice, the young man observed as the old man hit basket after basket. He was amazed that the old man could even dribble and get up and down the court in a wheelchair.

After attending a few more practices, the young man picked up a basketball and started shooting it. It wasn't long before he got better than the old man who decided to mentor him. They eventually went on to win the Wheelchair Basketball Championship. The young man learned team work, how to overcome limitations and a bad attitude, and most of all the willingness it takes to learn from a mentor.

Wow! I don't know about you, but I'm glad this older gentleman came into this young man's life. We all need mentors. I'm so glad and thankful for the wonderful people who have mentored me and changed my life.

They gave me the courage and willpower to go on regardless of my circumstances. They stood by my side and didn't abandon me when I needed them most. That's how I made it. They didn't give up on me.

SIX REASONS WHY YOU NEED A MENTOR

1. Mentors help you to solve problems and find solutions. They help guide and direct you when you're trying to make decisions. They listen

and give you advice only when it's necessary. Mentors can save you years of learning from their experience.

2. Mentors want you to succeed. They have a built-in passion to transfer information, wisdom, knowledge, and experience to help you succeed.

3. Mentors are willing to put up with your mistakes and failures. Mentors understand that you will sometimes make mistakes and have failures. They are willing to be patient with you until you mature and develop.

4. Mentors help you to prioritize your time, goals, and dreams. Mentors help you put first things first. They can help you stay focused on what's most important and eliminate what's not.

5. Mentors want commitment, not just effort. Many people pursue mentors for all types of reasons. It's your responsibility to pursue your mentors. You need to make a commitment to follow up on their instructions, training, and advice. Even if you don't agree with everything, just do it. Mentors want more than just effort; they want results.

6. Mentors are not threatened by your success. Why? Because there is a possibility you will become like them or exceed their accomplishments. It's a compliment to them! They want to see you release your greatness.

Recovering from a Failure

"Most successes have been built on failures, not on one failure alone but several. A man is never beaten until he thinks he is."

–Charles Gow

The statement above is so true. If you ask anyone who has been successful, they will tell you that it was accomplished by failing at various times in their lives. Thomas Edison said, "Many of life's failures are people who did not realize how close they were to success when they gave up."

What have you failed at? How many times did you fail? Did you try again? Or did you just quit and walk away?

The pursuit of greatness is a road full of challenges, struggles, hurts, and pains. The pursuit of greatness is full of disappointments and unforeseen setbacks.

What makes the pursuit of greatness worthwhile is, no matter how many times you fail, as long as you don't quit, you can recover and start all over again.

THE PURSUIT OF GREATNESS

George Foreman was considered one of the most feared Heavyweight Champion of the World back in 1974.

He went into the ring to fight Muhammad Ali, where George was heavily favored to win. Instead, Muhammad Ali knocked out George in the eighth round. His life would be hurled into a setback. George Foreman quit boxing.

For twenty years, he went through a recovery period before he stepping back into the ring in November of 1994 at the age of forty-five. Against all odds, he planned to recapture his boxing title and become Heavyweight Champion of the World once again.

George said, "They said I could never hope to get back into fighting shape. I was a hundred pounds heavier than when I won the title from Joe Frazier fourteen years before. They said the muscle memory I needed to throw a punch was lost forever, and what I aimed to do couldn't be done because, it hadn't been done."

George Foreman proved to all the doubters, skeptics, and press who said he was too old, they were wrong. He took a setback and learned from his failures. He gained experience and became Heavyweight Champion of the World, again. He recovered from a failure by winning at the end.

You, too, can recover from a setback. It could be bankruptcy, job loss, foreclosure, health issues, or income reduction. It doesn't matter. Failure is not final. You can bounce back. It's time for you to recover and proceed on your road to greatness.

PART 4

DISPLAYING YOUR GREATNESS

25 WAYS TO
RELEASE
THE
GREATNESS
IN YOU

CHAPTER SIXTEEN

Becoming Extraordinary

"Some people may have greatness thrust upon them. Very few have excellence thrust upon them. They achieve it."

–John Gardner

Have you ever wondered what separates the ordinary person from the extraordinary person? Or why one person can be given many things to do and succeed, while another person with only one thing to do, complains, criticizes, and refuses to cooperate to get the job done? The answer is, it's the "extra."

For you to release your greatness, you have to become extraordinary in everything you do. To simply try is not enough—you must excel.

EXTRAORDINARY!

That's how you describe a three-year-old girl from Kosciusko, Mississippi, reciting scripture at church. At age seventeen, she became Miss Fire Prevention in Nashville, Tennessee. She was hired at a local radio station because she impressed the managers with how well she read the news. Two years later, in her sophomore year at Tennessee State University, she became the first woman, and the first African-American woman, to anchor TV news in Nashville.

That was just the start for Oprah Winfrey, who has achieved greatness far beyond her humble beginnings. She has changed and impacted the lives of millions of people, who are touched by her love, sincerity, and genuinely caring spirit. That spirit has lifted many out of hopelessness, despair, poverty, and depression.

Oprah Winfrey stands out far above other people who just talk about making a difference. She does something about it. She gives millions of dollars to better humanity. She's raised millions of dollars through Oprah's Angel Network, and awards college scholarships.

"The Oprah Winfrey Show" has been the number-one talk show for more than twenty consecutive seasons and is seen on television by more than forty-nine million homes and 122 countries daily.

OPRAH'S EXTRAORDINARY ACHIEVEMENTS

- Oprah Winfrey made her acting debut in 1985 as Sofia in Steven Spielberg's The Color Purple for which she received both Academy Award and Golden Globe Nominations.

- In 1986, The Oprah Winfrey Show went into syndication and became the highest-rated talk show in television history.

- In 2000, she became magazine founder and editorial director of O, The Oprah Magazine, which is one of today's leading women's lifestyle publications.

- In 2002, she became television programming creator of Dr. Phil, a syndicated daytime talk show produced through Harpo Productions, Inc.

Oprah has truly shown what it means to become great by becoming a servant to all. She has taken all her hurt, pain, brokenness, and abuse, and used it to become an extraordinary person.

I'm so grateful to and thankful for Oprah Winfrey. This is a woman of high quality and character, who continues to defy all odds against her and becomes even greater.

This is how everyone should strive to live their lives—not for the good of themselves, but for the good of all mankind. To do so is to fulfill your greatness.

CHAPTER SEVENTEEN

Doing the Impossible

*"Few will have the greatness to bend history itself, but
each of us can work to change a small portion of events
... It is from numberless diverse acts of courage and belief
that human history is shaped."*

—Robert F. Kennedy

I hope you are starting to feel that releasing your
greatness is a journey. In this journey, you will face a
threat to your success called "impossible." This enemy's
voice may come from the inside of you, or it could come
from others who believe you just can't do it.

You must be determined within yourself that
impossible is not an option. It's not impossible to live
your dreams. It's not impossible to live a happy life. It's
not impossible to be healthy, wealthy, and live a long life.

DEFYING GREAT ODDS

Impossible! That's what was told to a young man
from Louisville, Kentucky, who shook up the world by
knocking out Sonny Liston in 1964. Cassius Clay won
boxing's title of Heavyweight Champion of the World.

Few people could match his charisma, wit,
and power to do the impossible. But Muhammad Ali
(formerly known as Cassius Clay), rewrote history.

Ali went into the fight with Sonny Liston as a 7-to-
1 underdog. He defied all the odds against him. He said

he was "The Greatest" and proved he was by becoming the greatest Heavyweight Champion who ever lived. However, the road to greatness for Ali would see many highs and lows over the next few years.

THE GREAT CONTROVERSY

Two days after the fight, Cassius Clay announced that he was converting to the Nation of Islam and that he changed his name to Muhammad Ali. The change was so controversial during the 1960s that the New York Times and several other newspapers refused to acknowledge his new name when writing about him.

On April 28, 1967, Ali made another controversial decision. The U.S. Army drafted him during the war in Vietnam; but he refused to go, saying it was against his religion.

Ali also asked why the government would want him to go fight in the war when he could pay the salaries of hundreds of soldiers. He was already paying the government $6 million in taxes. He said, "I aian't got a quarrel with them Viet Cong. No Viet Cong ever called me the 'N' word."

THE GREAT SETBACK

Ali was fined $10,000, sentenced to five years in prison, and stripped of his heavyweight title. He would spend the next two-and-a-half years in exile, but he became a national figure who spoke out against the war in Vietnam. He traveled to colleges and did theatrical plays to earn money the best way he could. Ali stood behind his convictions and never gave up hope.

That is what you have to do when you encounter a setback. You can't give up, no matter how difficult life gets. Setbacks will always appear throughout your lifetime, when you least expect them. You must prepare for your comeback.

THE GREAT COMEBACK

Ali's future seemed uncertain. Four years later, the U.S. Supreme Court overturned his conviction because of procedural grounds and granted him the right to obtain a license to box again.

In 1971, Muhammad Ali returned to the ring to fight Joe Frazier in what was billed as "The Fight of the Century." The fight took place in New York at Madison Square Garden. Ali lost.

The setback became a great comeback, as Muhammad Ali would go on to regain his heavyweight title against George Foreman in 1974, in hot Zaire, Africa. Ali was then a 3-to-1 underdog. It didn't matter.

Ali continued to solidify his greatness in history by beating Leon Spinks in 1978, during a return bout to win the heavyweight title for the third time. This was an accomplishment no other boxer did before him.

YOUR COMEBACK

I don't know what has thrown your life into a setback, but you can decide to get up off the canvas of life and not be counted out of the ring by developing your greatness.

I know there is a winner inside of you. I know there is a burning passion that drives you to live your dreams. Otherwise, you wouldn't be reading this book.

So today, do the impossible! Rewrite history. Be the first in your family, city, community, and nation to make a difference. Who knows? One day, people could be calling you "The Greatest."

CHAPTER EIGHTEEN

The Power of Serving Others

"Everybody can be great ... because anybody can serve. You don't have to have a college degree to serve. You don't have to make your subject and verb agree to serve ... You only need a heart full of grace, a soul generated by love."

—*Martin Luther King Jr.*

Sidney Powell summed up the power of serving others when he said, "Try to forget yourself in the service of others. For when we think too much of ourselves, and our own interest, we easily become despondent. But when we work for others, our efforts return to bless us."

BEING SERVED BY OTHERS

Have you ever gone to a restaurant and the sign said, "Please wait to be seated"? Then, you waited there patiently; but after a while, you became frustrated because nobody acknowledged you? And when you got to the table, you waited some more and finally a server walked up to you with a glass of water and said, "May I help you?" You probably told yourself that it was poor service, and that you won't be back.

Have you ever had to wait in line at a bank, go to the emergency room at a hospital, or stand in line while shopping, only to feel like those waiting on you didn't really care? What about customer service? Have you ever taken something back you purchased from a store, only to be treated rudely and spoken to harshly by the customer representative?

The power of serving others means to put yourself in other people's place and sincerely care about solving their problems or meeting their needs. Since I have worked in retail and with the public throughout my life, I know the importance of wearing a smile, showing interest, and being courteous and patient toward customers who have questions, concerns, or complaints.

What I really want to suggest is, if you are a person in any type of service business or organization who deals with the public, it's about them and not about you. I have seen people take a simple complaint from a customer and make it personal. Some displayed bad attitudes; others talked on the phone and made you wait deliberately or passed you on to someone else because they didn't want to serve you.

The power of serving others is to have a positive attitude. Give good service. Show that it's not beneath you to give of yourself, whether it's time, talent, energy, money, or even sacrifice to make someone else's life a little better.

A PASSION FOR SERVING OTHERS

Mother Teresa, one of the greatest people ever to serve others during her lifetime said, "Unless life is lived for others, it is not worthwhile."

As a young nun, Mother Teresa had a burning desire to work with people who were less fortunate, homeless, and hopeless. Her superiors were not convinced she could do it because they said she was too young and inexperienced.

As a result, Mother Teresa was assigned to teach at St. Mary's High School in Calcutta, India. Her mission to serve others never wavered. At thirty-nine years old, she was allowed to pursue her passion for those who were among the poorest of the poor, in the slums of Calcutta.

Mother Teresa started a school to teach the poor children in these slums. She had no funds, but depended on Divine Providence. She learned basic medicine and went into the homes to treat them.

On her first day in Calcutta, she met a man lying in the gutter. Everyone avoided him because he was covered with insects and sores. Mother Teresa knelt down to the man and he was so surprised that this nun would care for him. He asked her, "Why are you helping me?" Mother Teresa smiled and responded, "Because I love you."

YOU POSSESS THE POWER OF SERVING OTHERS

You may be working in health care, or for a bank or credit union. Your occupation could be a custodian, a waitress, a mechanic, a leader of a nonprofit organization, a volunteer, or a CEO of a major corporation. All of these jobs involve giving service to people or working with the public. Whatever your occupation, it's up to you to set the standard of showing humility and genuinely caring for people through the "power of serving others."

Go out of your way; remember to treat people how you want to be treated. Greatness has to be more than just obtaining status, popularity, money, fame, or the desire to be great. It is following a golden rule that says, "It's better to give than to receive." Make serving others your trademark. It truly is the secret to becoming great.

CHAPTER NINETEEN

Touch Others with Love

*"Love that lasts involves a real and genuine concern for
others as persons, for their values as they feel them, for their
development and growth."*

—Evelyn Duvall

Have you recognized the opportunity to touch the life of someone who needs your love? Somebody right now is hurting, lonely, depressed, broke, debt-ridden, or lacking friendship. You could be that companion or confidant who understands and cares for them. True greatness can only be demonstrated through love.

It must be genuine. It must be sincere. It must be powerful enough for you to give it away without being rewarded or compensated for it. Apostle Paul understood that "love" is the greatest force in the world. He wrote about it in a way that allows us to check out the real motives behind our love.

In I Corinthians 13:3–8 of the Contemporary English Version of the Bible, Apostle Paul says:

What if I gave away all that I owned and let myself be burned alive? I would gain nothing, unless I loved others. Love is kind and patient, never jealous, boastful, proud, or rude. Love isn't selfish or quick tempered. It doesn't keep a record of wrongs others do. Love rejoices in the truth, but not in evil. Love is always supportive, loyal, hopeful, and trusting. Love never fails.

All of these are important attributes to build your life around. It means that true love is not given for selfish ambitions or gain. Real love is not boastful, proud, or rude. It is a heartfelt appreciation and concern for others. Real love reaches out and touches others without any bias or prejudices.

Even if you are hurt or let down, love doesn't hold grudges or remind you of the past mistakes you have made. Love doesn't seek to get even. True love toward others is supportive, hopeful, and interested in the things they like. It's being loyal to those you love, even when other people won't give them a second chance. That is what it means to touch others with love. So find time today to give love away.

Jesus, Apostle Paul, along with Mother Teresa, Princess Diana, and Martin Luther King Jr. touched the world with love. What about you? You must recognize the opportunities that you have been given to love people unconditionally—with no strings attached. When you do, it's another stepping stone toward releasing your greatness.

CHAPTER TWENTY

Outwork Everyone Else And Over Deliver

"To be successful, you must outwork everyone else and over deliver every time."

—Earvin "Magic" Johnson

Have you ever wondered how some people make it to become a superstar? Is it talent alone? Is it intelligence? Being a genius? Think about some of the greatest performers, celebrities, leaders, or business people of all time. What made them great? What made them stand out above the crowd? What made them different?

A COMMITMENT TO GREATNESS

I believe a major part of it was outworking and over delivering better than anyone else. Understand that greatness comes with a price tag that few people are willing to pay. A lot of us have dreams, visions, and goals for ourselves, but some people are not willing to put in the extra work, hours, toil, sacrifice, or preparation it takes to release their greatness. Here's what I want to do in this chapter. I want to fire you up. I want to get you pumped up to the point that you take massive action to change your life. I want you to get unstuck, go forward, and stop making excuses. What I mean is, you have to start out-hustling and out-thinking others, by using strategies and systems that propel you beyond normal efforts.

You have to be more dedicated and committed to seeing yourself rise to the top. The best thing about preparing to release the greatness in you is the person you become. It's the mindset you adopt as a winner. It's the joy and satisfaction of knowing that you gave it your best. Bad circumstances couldn't stop you. Unforeseen tragedies couldn't hold you back. Childhood scars and hurts couldn't limit you. People with wrong motives and injustice couldn't break you down.

FROM NBA GREAT TO BILLION-DOLLAR BUSINESSMAN

Awesome! What more can you say about Earvin "Magic" Johnson who dazzled fans and players for thirteen seasons in the NBA with his skills and charisma? He won five NBA Championships. He was named as one of the 50 greatest players and is in the Basketball Hall of Fame.

Since retiring from playing and coaching professional basketball in 1995, Earvin "Magic" Johnson is now a business tycoon with over 110 Starbucks; six Magic Johnson Theaters; 31 Burger King restaurants; 12 fitness centers; and $1 billion worth of real estate projects in urban markets across the country.

Magic was in Detroit some time ago to share his entrepreneurial wisdom to a group of students at Bizdom U, a two-year boot camp program for budding urban entrepreneurs, created by Dan Gilbert of Quicken Loans.

RICH AND FAMOUS DOESN'T EQUAL BUSINESS SUCCESS

Magic quickly dispelled the assumptions of the students who thought that being a rich and famous basketball player would make it easy to start a successful business career.

Magic stated, "My first business venture was a flop." It was a sports paraphernalia store in Los Angeles, in which he put $100,000. He was the sole owner, buyer, etc.

Johnson said, "I went out and bought 10 of this, 50 of that—came back and put it all in the store, and nothing sold for a month." The reason why is because he bought everything he liked, not what the customers liked.

It was a $100,000 lesson for Magic Johnson. His latter businesses have been successful because he made it his business to do his research and find out what the consumer wants.

Since then, he has chosen good business partners and worked like crazy. He doesn't hire clock-watchers. He said, "In today's business world, you must outwork everybody else and out-deliver them. Delivering isn't good enough."

The greatness you want to achieve will require you to out-perform, out-strategize, and out-deliver everyone else. Ready? On your mark, get set, go!

PART 5

PASSING ON YOUR GREATNESS

25 WAYS TO
RELEASE
THE
GREATNESS
IN YOU

CHAPTER TWENTY-ONE

Become a Bridge to Make Someone Else Great

"Too many times we look at greatness as what people accomplish individually, but true greatness is when you can become a bridge to make someone else great."

−Randy D. Wright

I have had the wonderful opportunity to work for major corporations, nonprofit operations, and Fortune 500 companies. I have been a part of organizations that teach people how to start their own business, purchase real estate, handle financial planning, tackle public speaking, as well as teach leadership and life skills to youth and adults. Yet in all my contacts with them, the one thing that I learned and observed is that they knew how to raise up leaders, invest in their employees, upgrade their skills, and enhance their performance. That is what made these corporations and businesses so successful to me.

In doing so, the companies became a bridge, created loyalty and trust, and boosted employee morale. In other words, these corporations were willing to share their vision, goals, and dreams with individuals who had these companies' interests at heart and in return, they helped make them great.

EMPOWERING OTHERS FOR GREATNESS

From a young age, I have always been a team player. Caring about people and working toward their success really matters to me. One instance, when I was a team leader with a manufacturing engineering plastics company, really stands out as an example.

I had five workers—four from a temporary agency and one full-time employee. The four temporary employees came to me and said, "Randy, whatever it takes for you to succeed, we are willing to help you." Wow! Needless to say, that gave me a boost of confidence and I had the courage to lead my team.

First, I made one of the workers, who was good at any job he undertook, my floor person and taught him everything I knew. I told him that he should always strive to be the best he can be and learn how the department runs—just in case he ever had the opportunity to be a team leader. I said, "I'm willing to invest in you."

GREATNESS PRODUCES RESULTS

This employee was elated that I would take the time to teach him what I knew and give him an opportunity to be successful. Eventually, he was promoted to another department within the company. I also had the privilege of producing four other team leaders. In addition, I was promoted three times within six months because I was willing to invest in others.

Here's my point: I never at one time felt threatened or worried that any of them were going to take my job. I wanted them to succeed because they were willing to give 100 percent to make sure that our team succeeded.

I know this goes against a lot of the traditional thinking of those who are scared or afraid of other people taking their jobs; but in reality, that is what all great people do. They see the potential, hunger, desire, and drive of certain individuals who are willing to pay the price of becoming successful and they help them achieve success.

What about you? Will you just remain a supervisor or manager who is comfortable with having other people follow you to make you look great? Or are you willing to become a bridge to help someone else become great? Why don't you start today by making a recommendation, giving a promotion, or putting in a good word to help jump-start somebody else's career.

Actor Danny Thomas said, "Success in life has nothing to do with what you gain in life or accomplish for yourself. It's what you do for others." So remember to become a bridge, not a stumbling block. You could be the difference maker that somebody's been waiting for.

CHAPTER TWENTY-TWO

Counting Up the Cost

"If you don't invest very much, then defeat doesn't hurt very much and winning is not very exciting."

—Dick Vermeil

Have you ever wanted something so badly that, whatever it took, you got it? Have you ever spent money on something you regretted buying and had to take it back later because you couldn't afford it? Have you ever made a major purchase after being pressured by a salesperson? If so, when you got home, were you frustrated because you didn't count up the cost?

COUNTING UP THE COST OF GREATNESS

When you decide to release your greatness, you have to count up the cost. You have to determine what price you are willing to pay. Guess what? The price won't be cheap.

- Greatness is a mindset that thinks and believes beyond normal circumstances.

- Greatness is giving your greatest performance when good is not enough.

- Greatness is living beyond your fears and overcoming personal limitations and struggles.

- Greatness is investing in your talents, gifts, and

abilities, and then demanding a return on them.

- Greatness makes you more than a conqueror if you don't quit and give up.

DO YOU HAVE WHAT IT TAKES?

Answer the following questions:

1. Why do you want to become great?
2. What characteristics make you qualified to become great?
3. Do you have the heart of a servant?
4. Do you have the heart of a champion?
5. Do you have the discipline and fortitude it takes to become great?
6. Are you willing to learn from mentors and others who are already great?

If you answered "no" to any of these questions, then maybe you have not counted up the cost of what it takes to become great.

LEARNING TO BECOME GREAT

Greatness has to be developed over time. It's a learning process. Some of the greatest achievers, record setters, and "movers and shakers" of the world had to learn to be great.

Bill Davison was a Michigan billionaire industrialist and owner of the three-time NBA World Champion Detroit Pistons, and the three-time WNBA Champion Detroit Shock. When he decided to purchase the Detroit Pistons thirty-six years ago, he never could have considered the wild ride ahead in his pursuit of owning a professional sports team. It all started when his dear friend Oscar Feldman, who was also his business partner and attorney, struck a conditional deal to buy the Pistons.

IS GREATNESS WORTH THE COST?

The framework of the deal took place when Bill Davidson and Fred Zollner, former owner of the Pistons, were walking along the Atlantic Ocean in Golden Beach, Florida. At the time, $6 million was the set price to purchase the Pistons.

Oscar Feldman flew down to Florida and shook hands on the deal that was subject to his due diligence. Feldman also went to Fort Wayne, Indiana, where he spent two days to review all of the Pistons' books and financial records.

He came away with a decision to tell Bill Davison not to buy the team. The cost wasn't worth the risk because the Pistons hadn't turned a profit in seventeen years of their existence.

Feldman told Davidson he would be happy to close the deal, but he didn't want any part of it.

TAKING THE RISK OF GREATNESS

Bill Davidson, who had other plans, convinced Feldman that they were still going to take the risk. He wanted Feldman to take a piece of ownership so he could look after the store for him.

Davidson's success didn't come quickly. For nearly ten years, there didn't appear to be any positive signs. After enduring horrible season after horrible season, Bill Davidson drafted Isiah Thomas in 1981. Three years later, the Pistons were in the playoffs.

The risk of producing a great franchise finally paid off in the 1989–1990 season, when the Pistons won their second NBA Championship, which was back-to-back. The Pistons also won an NBA Championship in 2004 by beating the Hall of Fame, star-studded Los Angeles Lakers, four games to one.

Bill Davidson's original investment of $6 million is now worth $469 million, according to Forbes Magazine. All of this because Bill Davidson was willing to stick it out and see his dream of greatness come to life.

He counted up the cost and took a risk. He was willing to face periods of isolation and criticism from people who thought he had made a big mistake. You, too, can rise to greatness by counting up the cost.

CHAPTER TWENTY-THREE

Turning Your Life into a Masterpiece through Crisis

"Crisis is an experience—not a final act. It's what you become through a crisis that turns your life into a masterpiece."

—Randy D. Wight

Priceless! That's what you are. You are one special, talented, and gifted person whose value exceeds a price tag. Think about it. Your mind is the most priceless possession you have. You use it to think, comprehend, create, memorize, study, solve problems, and store information.

Your life is like a masterpiece. Every day that you spend time working on releasing the greatness in you displays its beauty in the making.

A MASTERPIECE IN THE MAKING

What turns your life into a masterpiece? It's this very thing called life.

The everyday events of your life turn it into a masterpiece. Let me explain. Each person will have a series of struggles, pain, grief, trouble, and brokenness. It is through the series of tests and trials that each person is transformed into a work of art. I want you to stop getting upset at the first sign of trouble. I want you to relax and avoid going into depression if you have more bills to pay than you have money. You may be saying, "If I get one more call from a bill collector, if I get another shut-off notice, I'm going to lose it." No, you don't have to lose it. Be at peace within yourself, regain your composure, learn from it, and let it make you into a masterpiece.

Now you might be saying, "You just don't understand what I'm going through. How is this present situation going to get better unless I react to it?"

That's the problem. Every time you react negatively to a problem or crisis you will get a negative result. Have you ever been at a utility company to pay your bill and witnessed another customer come in angry and upset, cursing out the service representative? It only made matters worse, didn't it?

It may feel good temporarily to give others a "piece of your mind," but it doesn't solve the problem.

GETTING THE RIGHT RESULTS

Here's my point: I have been in situations where my gas and lights were about to be shut off. But it was my response, not my reaction that got results.

When I had to meet with the service representatives, I explained my situation and sought to work out payment arrangements. They agreed and put me on a monthly budget plan—problem solved.

However, there was a time, because of financial difficulties, that I could not meet my obligations and they shut off my gas and lights. That time, my first reaction was, "You can't work with me? You don't understand that things are hard right now." I was embarrassed, humiliated, and upset. I didn't tell anyone.

Then, I realized that I was getting too upset. I said, "Why am I reacting negatively to a negative situation?" I began to calm down and resolve that this was not going to defeat me. I made up my mind that the situation was not going to depress me or get me all stressed out. It was then that I discovered that my inner peace was greater than my outward circumstances. Eventually, my service was restored and everything went back to normal.

That's what your life being a masterpiece in the making means. When you can go through and survive all of life's ups and downs without letting it break you, that's adding a stroke of greatness to your life.

When you start to understand that every crisis, hardship, or letdown you survive makes you priceless, you gain experience. You build up patience and fortitude. You gain wisdom and understanding.

But most of all, you can tell somebody else that is experiencing the same things you went through that you made it. And they can make it, too.

Crisis comes to make you strong not weak. Crisis sometimes happens unexpectedly and gives you no warning. So, enjoy the ride as you began to see your life unfold before your eyes. You are a masterpiece—a jewel—and that makes you priceless.

A CHILDHOOD CRISIS

Dave Thomas, founder of Wendy's restaurants, was adopted at six months old by a couple from Michigan. His adoptive mother died when he was only five years old.

Dave's adoptive father was a construction worker who married three more times. Dave received love and stability from his father and later started his first job at twelve. At fifteen, Dave quit school in the tenth grade to work in the restaurant business full-time.

Dave worked his way up from a busboy to a manager in a family restaurant. That's where he met the famous

Colonel Sanders of Kentucky Fried Chicken (KFC). Colonel Sanders mentored Thomas, which led him to purchase a string of failing KFC restaurants in 1962. Six years later, Dave was a millionaire at age thirty-five.

FROM ADOPTION TO ENTREPRENEUR

The money Thomas made allowed him to open his first Wendy's Old Fashioned Hamburgers restaurant in 1969 in Columbus, Ohio. Wendy's was named after Dave's daughter Melinda Lou, whose nickname was Wendy. Thomas admitted that his initial goal was only to open up one restaurant. He said, "I could eat for free."

Dave Thomas revolutionized the fast-food business. He insisted on fresh ground beef, not frozen hamburgers. Dave was asked several times throughout his life why Wendy's hamburgers were square. He replied, "Because we don't cut corners."

A MASTERPIECE IN THE MAKING

Dave hated being labeled as a "fast-food" business. His earlier Wendy's restaurants had carpeted dining rooms, Bentwood chairs, Tiffany style lamps, and news-print tabletops. Wendy's was the first food chain to add a drive-through window and a salad bar to its restaurants.

In 1995, Wendy's merged with Tim Hortons, Canada's largest coffee and baked goods chain. Together, they have more than 2,000 shops and their sales exceed $8 billion annually. When Dave Thomas died on January 8, 2002, there were more than 6,000 Wendy's restaurants worldwide, in more than thirty countries.

A CRISIS TURNS INTO A GREAT CAUSE FOR ADOPTED KIDS

It wasn't until the late 1980s that Dave Thomas said he felt ashamed that he didn't speak out about adoption before, even though he was adopted.

Dave's message about success isn't dependent upon coming from a privileged background; his story shows that anyone can do it. It motivated one of his managers to tell Dave to make the public aware of the importance of adoption as well as finding homes for children in foster care. Dave's listened and became a national advocate for adopted children.

As I was visiting a Wendy's one day, I noticed a poster of Dave as a child, at eight years old. The thing about the picture that stood out to me the most was Dave's words about his commitment to see families come together, share special moments, and build better communities.

Dave Thomas was a wonderful example of the process it takes to develop into greatness. You have to enjoy the process as you develop into your greatness. How committed are you?

Kenneth Blanchard said, "There's a difference between interest and commitment. When you're interested in doing something, you do it only when it's convenient. When you're committed to something, you accept no excuses; only results."

CHAPTER TWENTY-FOUR

Leaving a Legacy for Future Generations

"We must not only give what we have, we must also give what we are."

–Cardinal Mercier

What legacy will you leave for the next generation? Who will you mentor and prepare to be great in the future? Whose greatness matters to you the most? This is the very foundation for 25 Ways to Release the Greatness in You.

YOUR GREATNESS HAS TO EXPAND BEYOND YOUR LIFETIME

Preparing the next generation to release their greatness has to start with you. People can no longer sit back and complain about how bad times are and not train, mentor, and develop the next decade of entrepreneurs, mayors, governors, presidents, educators, and responsible fathers and mothers.

- You have the power to make a difference.
- You have the power to bring about change.
- Are you willing to leave a legacy that is still standing when you're gone?

I hope you are up to the task because the world needs men, women, fathers, mothers, teenagers, boys, and girls who are willing to live a life that's bigger than what they can imagine for themselves. You can help make others great!!!

CREATING A LEGACY

Every mother or father who has poured into the lives of their children, teaching them good principles, morals, manners, and respect for themselves and others, is leaving a legacy for future generations.

Every teacher who has taught young people math, science, biology, history, English, reading, and writing is leaving a legacy for future generations.

Every mentor who has passed on their wisdom, knowledge, and skills to their mentees is leaving a legacy for future generations.

Every doctor, lawyer, engineer, mechanic, plumber, electrician, or pharmacist who is training an apprentice to own his or her own business or practice is leaving a legacy for future generations.

Every leader who is leading people to reach their full potential and release the greatness in them is leaving a legacy for future generations.

THE FORGOTTEN LEGACY

When I think about all of the great people who have changed history; created successful inventions; broke records; won Grammy Awards, Academy Awards, and gold medals; and have left a legacy for future generations to follow, I think about all the mothers and grandmothers who have had to keep the families together and raise kids in single homes. Yet they get very little recognition or credit when it comes to leaving a legacy for future generations. I want to thank each of you "GREAT WOMEN"; for without you, there would be no legacies.

CREATING A FAMILY LEGACY

My dad Troy Wright Jr. and my mom Catherine Wright Hall started a family legacy well before I was born.

My mom is the second oldest of nine children. She had to start out at an early age helping her mother to raise her brothers and sisters. She learned how to cook at eight years old. Many days, she had to carry and wash clothes in a dangerous secluded area in the South.

Mom shared some stories with me that she learned and experienced as a child. I would like to share some of her stories with you. She said, "When you are brought up and you are poor, life can be very difficult."

Mom's dad was a coal miner and sometimes he would go days without work. This put their family under extreme financial pressure, as her parents had to make ends meet.

Mom could not finish school after the sixth grade. Though she had many chores and responsibilities, one of Mom's favorite times was when her mother would bring home magazines.

Mom loved reading the stories and looking at the pictures. This is where her love for reading came from and it eventually led to her reading many books. She became very knowledgeable in science, medicine, history, the Bible, animals, and the human body. This is a legacy she passed on to all of us, as all of her children love to read books and magazines.

THINKING ABOUT HER FUTURE FAMILY

Some of Mom's most memorable times were when

she took care of her brothers and sisters. She used those experiences as building blocks for starting her own family.

She would tell herself that one day, when she had her own children, she would make sure that they would never walk around barefooted or have running noses. She said that lying, stealing, and cheating would not be the characteristics that she would build her family upon. It just wasn't going to be a part of her children's lives. Teaching her children how to have good manners and act in public were high on her priority list.

The thing that stands out the most to me about my mother is that she was determined to create a legacy for her family. She decided to set the standard of excellence that each of her children would pass on to their sons and daughters when the time came.

The small coal-mining town where she grew up had people from various backgrounds. A lot of times the people got drunk and behaved in ways that displeased Mom. She also made up her mind that when she became an adult she would not behave like that or raise a family that behaved like that. Mom said, "I will not let my behavior exceed the limit of being responsible for raising my children."

HOW TO LEAVE A FAMILY LEGACY

My grandmother passed these morals and characteristics on to Mom, who passed them on to me and my family. For instance, when she became a preteen-ager, a guy wanted to take her to the movies. The first thing he asked is for her to have sex with him. My grandmother said that's all he wanted. My grandmother Lucille Yancey instilled the importance of her being a young lady first and not lowering her standards to somebody else's.

Mom passed this on my sisters Rosie, Beatrice, and

Kathy. She taught them how to be young ladies who were not loose and how to not be persuaded by guys who only had one thing on their minds—to "hit it and quit it."

She told my brother and me not do anything to somebody's daughter that we wouldn't want done to our sisters. She urged me and my brother to wait until we got married to have sex and not to bring any babies in her house because she wasn't going to take care of them. Mom made each of her children make a commitment to graduate from high school and bring home that diploma—no exceptions!

Mom taught her children the importance of reading and writing because her mother couldn't read and write—and people took advantage of her many times for that. Talking properly, showing respect to adults, and having etiquette were very important to Mom. She wanted her children to know how to handle and conduct themselves in public. So, learning how to set a table and to use the right fork were huge to her.

Overall, Mom stressed the importance of being a leader—not following everybody else. I often remember her saying, "If you are going to let somebody else use your mind, what's the since in having one?"

Here, Mom has agreed to share her top ten tips for being a successful parent, which is one of the most important places to begin releasing a person's greatness.

TEN TIPS FOR BEING SUCCESSFUL A PARENT

1. Your child is looking to you for what they need in terms of guidance and direction. Give it to them.

2. Never neglect your child. You have to be there for them.

3. As a young parent, it's easy to want to enjoy life,

party, and be a teenager. That's to be expected but not when you are leaving your child with other people. You have to be there for your child.

4. Don't beat up your child with abusive words.

5. Tell your children how special and important they are.

6. Tell them they can do anything they set their minds to do.

7. Don't ever allow the words "you can't" to be a part of their lives. Say "you can."

8. One of the greatest gifts in life is to be a mother. So never regret it.

9. If you really love your children, love them unconditionally with no strings attached. Don't say, "If you do this, then I will do that."

10. If you have not finished [high] school because you had children, go back and get your GED.

Moma got her G.E.D. at the age of 45. Wow! What words of wisdom and understanding from a young woman who married at sixteen years old and had a baby at seventeen years old. She knows from experience what it takes to raise a family and be a wife, grandmother, and great-grandmother. I hope this has helped you to understand the importance of leaving a legacy for future generations.

My family has successful business owners, social workers, therapists, ministers, college graduates, professional chefs, teachers, motivational speakers, poets, writers, entrepreneurs, and now the first published author. All of this was made possible through the dream of a young girl who decided that greatness was to be the standard set for her immediate family and future generations to come.

That is what I want you to do. Think beyond your immediate family. Think in terms of impacting and influencing future generations now. The preparation of future generations must begin today—not tomorrow.

CHAPTER TWENTY-FIVE

The Formula for Greatness

"One of the most difficult things everyone has to learn is that for your entire life you must keep fighting and adjusting if you hope to survive. No matter who you are or what your position you must keep fighting for whatever it is you desire to achieve."

–George Allen

The formula for greatness is to be used alongside the many different experiences and events that happen in our lives. Consider some of the following scenarios.

GREATNESS COMES IN MANY FORMS

To be told by a doctor that you have a negative physical condition that you will have to live with for the rest of your life, but you refuse to let it make you bitter, resentful, or mean. That's greatness!!!

To lose your home due to foreclosure from the loss of a job, which forces you to live with relatives or downsize to an apartment or townhouse can be depressing. Yet you choose to handle this as a temporary setback instead of feeling like a failure. That's greatness!!!

To be a single parent with the responsibility of raising your children due to divorce or death of a spouse, with little or no government assistance can be frightening. But you are determined to make it, regardless of low income, lack of health care, and aging parents. That's greatness!!!

To be a new entrepreneur with no guarantee of business success because the law of averages says that most start-up businesses fail within the first five years is a daunting prospect. Yet you keep on planning, persevering, working, networking, and investing in your business until it finally makes a profit. That's greatness!!!

I want to encourage anyone who has ever had to struggle with issues, problems, pain, and people that seemed too great to overcome, but you made it in spite of them. I applaud you because it's easy to quit when life get's hard. It's easy to blame other people for where you are in life. It's easy to hold grudges and keep unforgiveness in your heart because someone has hurt you and done you wrong.

Don't ever let those hurtful experiences stop you. When you survive all that life throws at you, no matter how difficult times are, no matter how nerve-racking or earth-shattering it seems, on the other side of it you can say, "I made it. The storms of life didn't take me out!"

You didn't die. You didn't lose your mind. You became stronger. You are a winner. You have what it takes to be great, think great, and do great things. That's what it means to release the greatness in you.

In closing, I want to share The Formula for Greatness with you. Use it earnestly!

THE FORMULA FOR GREATNESS

G—Give it all you've got.

> *Greatness doesn't just happen; you have to give it all you've got. Just keep going forward. You can never reach your destination by standing still.*

R—Reach for a brighter tomorrow.

Reach for the best, create the future you desire, and let faith empower you on your journey to greatness.

E—Enter each day with enthusiasm.

Enthusiasm is the spark plug that drives you to complete what you have started. It is the energy booster you need each day.

A—Achieve the very best for you and your family.

You must create a lifestyle of achievement and accomplishments that will leave a legacy for you and your family. Eric Butterworth said, "Nothing stops the man who desires to achieve. Every obstacle is simply a course to develop his achievement muscle. It's strengthening his powers of accomplishment."

T—Touch and inspire those who need it most.

Never forget that you are an inspiration to somebody. Be sensitive to those around you who need a word of encouragement or someone to lift them up.

N—Never quit. The release of your greatness will happen.

Great things take time to happen. It's a process that involves a series of tests and trials.

E—Excellence.

Excellence is taking "greatness" to another level. Become the best at what you do. Remember, average and ordinary are not options.

S—Stability is soundness inside out.

You must remain stable in the midst of any crisis. Soundness is the foundation for overcoming any obstacles stacked against you.

S—Stay focused and fired up about life.

Staying focused and fired up is 99 percent of winning the battles in your life. Don't let anything or anyone distract you from reaching your greatness. Remember, broken focus is just a distraction disguised as an opportunity.

There you have it - a complete system for releasing the Greatness in You. Apply it to every area of your life.

REMEMBER...

- You are Greatness in the Making
- Developing a New Mindset
- Releasing Your Greatness
- Displaying your Greatness
- Passing on your Greatness to Future Generations

Credits and Sources
Of Information from Randy D. Wright

Chapter 1
"Janice Bryant Howroyd"
Source: ©2002 Essence 50 of the Most Inspiring African Americans.

Chapter 2
Thomas Watson, Sr. was a man of vision. He built IBM (International Business Machines) into the world's largest manufacturer of electric typewriters and data processing equipment.
Source: Speaker's Source Book ©1994

Chapter 3
Bucky Fuller
Source: Speaker's Source Book ©1994
He is best known as the inventor of the geodesic dome—a building that could sustain its own weight with no practical limits. It is the lightest, strongest and most cost-effective structure ever devised.
Bucky went on to become a world-famous engineer, mathematician, architect, philosopher and poet. He held more than 170 patents before his death in 1983.

Chapter 4
"Charles Darrow" Inventor of the Game Monopoly
Source: Speaker's Source Book ©1994

Chapter 5
Dr. Sampson Davis is an emergency room physician; Dr. George Jenkins is a dentist; and Dr. Rameck Hunt is an internist. Oprah Winfrey called the three doctors "the premier role models of the world." They have written two books on the New York Times best-seller list called The Pact and We Beat the Street.
Source: ©2002 Essence 50 of the Most Inspiring African Americans.

Chapter 6
"Scotty Pippen NBA Player
Source: ©NBA.com

Chapter 7
"Henry Ward Beecher"
Source: Speaker's Source Book ©1994

Chapter 8
"Dr. Suess, Alex Haley, Charles Goodyear, Paul Elrich,
Source: Speaker's Source Book ©1994 and Sally Jessy Raphael Bio

Chapter 9
"Leo Gerstenzang" Inventor of Q-Tips, Madame CJ Walker, King C. Gillett, Ole Evinrude, Charles Strite inventor of the
Automatic pop up toaster,
Source: Speaker's Source Book ©1994

Chapter 10
"Debbie Fields" Mrs. Fields Cookies
Source: Success Magazine © 2006

Chapter 11
"Joseph" in Bible Genesis 37-42
Source: ©1995 American Bible Society

Chapter 12
"My Own Story"
Source: Randy D. Wright ©2011

Chapter 13
"Norman Vincent Peele"
Source: Speaker's Source Book © 1994

Chapter 14
"The Young Skier"
Source: Speaker's Source Book ©1994

Chapter 15
"George Foreman"
Source: Success Magazine ©2006

Chapter 16
"Oprah Winfrey"
Source: ©Bio on internet

Chapter 17
"Muhammad Ali"
Source: ©Biography on line.

Chapter 18
"Mother Teresa"
Source: Speaker's Source Book ©1994

Chapter 19
"I Corinthians 13:3-8
Source: C.E.V. Bible ©1995 American Bible Society

Chapter 20
"Earvin Magic Johnson"
Source: ©Detroit Free Press

Chapter 21
"My own story"
Source: Randy D. Wright ©2011

Chapter 22
"Bill Davison" Piston Owner
Source: ©Piston's.com and ©Detroit Free Press

Chapter 23
"Dave Thomas"
Source: Speaker's Source Book ©1994

Chapter 24
"Leaving A Legacy For Future Generations
Source: Catherine Wright Hall and Randy D. Wright ©2011

Chapter 25
"The Formula for Greatness"
Source: Randy D. Wright ©2011

62282160R00076

Made in the USA
Lexington, KY
03 April 2017